G000088723

Corn

TARLA DALAL

India's # 1 Cookery Author

S&C

SANJAY & CO.

MUMBAI

Price: Rs. 89/-

Published & Distributed by : **Sanjay & Company**

353/A-1, Shah & Nahar Industrial Estate, Dhanraj Mill Compound, Lower Parel (W), Mumbai - 400 013. INDIA.
Tel. : (91-22) 2496 8068 ● Fax : (91-22) 2496 5876 ● E-mail : sanjay@tarladalal.com

Printed by : **Minal Sales Agencies**, Mumbai

UK and USA customers can call us on :

UK : 02080029533 ● USA : 213-634-1406

For books, Membership on **tarladalal.com**, Subscription for **Cooking & More** and Recipe queries
Timing : 9.30 a.m. to 7.00 p.m. (IST), from Monday to Saturday
Local call charges applicable

Recipe Research &
Production Design
Arati Fedane
Umaima Abdullally

Nutritionists
Nisha Katira
Sapna Kamdar

Food Styling
Shubhangi Dhaimade

Photography
Jignesh Jhaveri

Typesetting
Adityas Enterprises

Designed by
Satyamangal Rege

Copy Editing
Janani Gopalakrishnan

BULK PURCHASES : Tarla Dalal Cookbooks are ideal gifts. If you are interested in buying more than 500 assorted copies of Tarla Dalal Cookbooks at special prices, please contact us at 91-22-2496 8068 or email : sanjay@tarladalal.com

INTRODUCTION

Dear friends,

Some foods generally trigger nostalgic memories. Take, *bhutta*, for instance. It brings back fond memories of walking in the rain, standing around the *bhuttawalla's sigri* while he roasted it to perfection, and spiked it with salt, chilli powder and *nimbu*.

Corn has always been my all-time favourite food. There are various types of corn available in the market today, ranging from **white corn** also known as Indian corn or Flint corn, to the immensely popular **American corn**, which is yellow in colour and softer than white corn. Though some recipes in the book ask for white corn or yellow corn in particular, you can usually substitute one for the other based on availability and convenience. **Baby corn**, which is fast gaining popularity in India and world over, is obtained by harvesting the corn plant early. They are usually eaten whole and maintain their texture and flavour when cooked.

And now that all these varieties of corn are available throughout the year, both fresh and canned, you can enjoy them in many different ways. Keeping this in mind I present to you **'CORN'** a delightful book full of scrumptious and easy-to-follow corn recipes. This book comprises of a selection of Indian and International corn recipes including favorites like **Sweet Corn Soup** and **Grilled Corn Toast,** and some new and exciting recipes such as **Cheesy Corn Rawa Waffles** and **Corn Pulao**. The **forty-four corn recipes** in this book are divided course-wise into **six sections**, for easy reference.

5

'Starters and Cocktail Snacks', consists of recipes like Corn Fondue, Baby Corn Fritters and the ever-favorite Cheese Corn Balls. **'Soups'** includes a collection of delectable corn soups from around the world, including Corn Chowder, Corn Tortilla Soup and *Makai Shorba*. **'Salads'** comprises of some quick and easy-to-make corn salads. The main course is divided into two sections: **'Indian Corn Dishes'** which includes interesting *subzis* and rice dishes such as Baby Corn *Hara Masala* and *Corn Pulao* and **'International Corn Dishes'**, which is flooded with innovative recipes such as Baked Corn Sandwich, Corn Manchurian and Creamy Corn Pizza. **'Day-to-Day Corn Snacks'** includes yummy yet simple snack recipes like Corn *Sev Puris*, and Corn and Cottage Cheese Tacos, to satisfy those sudden hunger attacks.

So, put on your apron, roll up your sleeves and surprise your family and friends with these wonderful corn dishes!

Warm Regards,

CONTENTS

Starters & Cocktail Snacks

Cheesy Corn Fondue 9

Thai Sweet Corn Cutlets 11

Cheese Corn Balls 14

Baby Corn Fritters 16

Stuffed Potato Skins 18

Corn, Spinach and Rice Balls 22

Spicy Baby Corn 24

Crispy Corn Cups 26

Soups

Corn Chowder 28

Nacho Soup 30

Sweet Corn Soup 32

Green Pea Corn Soup 34

Corn, Basil and Fusilli Soup 36

Spinach and Baby Corn Soup 39

Makai Shorba 40

Salads

Mexican Bean and Cheese Salad 42

Burnt Corn Salad 44

Baby Corn and Mushroom Salad 46

Chatpata Salad 48

Indian Corn Dishes

Baby Corn Hara Masala 49

Corn Curry 51

7

Makai Paatal Bhaji 53

Methi Makai 56

Palak Baby Corn 58

Palak Makai Khaas 60

Corn Pulao 62

International Corn Dishes

Baby Corn and Soya Stir-Fry 64

Baked Corn Sandwich 67

Corn Manchurian 69

Steamed Curry Rice 71

Oriental Rice Noodles 73

Creamy Corn Pizza 76

Farfel with Baby Corn and
Walnuts...78

Chinese Vegetables in Hot Garlic
Sauce 80

Day to Day Corn Snacks

Cheesy Corn Rawa Waffles 82

Makai ni Khichdi 84

Corn And Cottage Cheese Tacos 87

Satay Sticks 89

Corn Sev Puris 91

Pearly Corn 93

Paneer and Corn Burger 95

Cheesy Corn Stuffed Jacket
Potatoes 97

Corn Panki 99

Grilled Corn Toasts 101

STARTERS & COCKTAIL SNACKS

🌾 *Cheesy Corn Fondue* 🌾

Picture on page 1.

Ideally fondue is so delectably thick that it does not drip from a bread cube dipped into it. Break away from the clichéed bread cubes, and serve this cheesy corn fondue with blanched vegetables such as carrot sticks or broccoli florets, instead.

Preparation time: 15 minutes.   Cooking time: 5 minutes.   Serves 6.

¾ cup cooked tender sweet corn kernels (*makai ke dane*), slightly crushed
¼ cup chopped onions
¼ tsp thinly sliced jalapenos
1 level tbsp plain flour (*maida*)
½ cup milk
¾ cup grated Parmaesean cheese
¼ cup grated mozzarella cheese
1 tbsp chopped olives

9

1 tbsp butter
Salt and freshly ground pepper to taste

For serving
Broken bread sticks
Toasted bread cubes
Broken cream crackers
Blanched vegetable sticks

1. Heat the butter in a pan, add the onions and sauté till they turn translucent.
2. Add the jalapenos and fry for a few seconds.
3. Add the flour and fry again for a minute.
4. Add the corn, milk, 1 cup of water and both the types of cheese and olives and cook until the mixture becomes thick.
5. Add the salt and pepper, mix well and pour into a fondue pot.
6. Serve hot. Let your guests serve themselves by dipping the bread sticks, toasted bread cubes, cream crackers or vegetable sticks into the hot fondue using forks or skewers.

Handy tip: If you do not have jalapenos, use ¼ tsp chopped green chillies instead.

❧ *Thai Sweet Corn Cutlets* ❧

Sweet corn cutlets, Thai style! Hot, sour, sweet and spicy everything you can ever wish for.

Preparation time: 20 minutes.   Cooking time: 20 minutes.   Serves 4.

For the cutlets
1½ cups tender sweet corn kernels (*makai ke dane*)
2 tbsp red curry paste, recipe below
2 tbsp soya sauce
¼ cup rice flour (*chawal ka atta*)
Salt to taste
Oil for greasing and deep-frying

For the red curry paste
5 whole dry red chillies, soaked in warm water for 10 minutes and drained
¼ cup chopped onions
4 cloves garlic
½ tbsp grated ginger

1 stalk lemon grass (*hari chai ka patta*), chopped
3 stalks coriander (only stalks not the leaves)
½ tbsp coriander (*dhania*) seeds
1 tbsp cumin seeds (*jeera*)
5-6 peppercorns
¼ tsp salt

For the hot and sweet dip
2 tbsp vinegar
¾ cup sugar
1 tbsp dry red chilli flakes
1 tbsp salt

For the red curry paste
Grind all the ingredients to a smooth paste in a mixer using a little water if required. Keep aside.

For the hot and sweet dip
1. Combine the vinegar, sugar and 1 cup of water in a pan and boil till the mixture becomes a thick syrup.

2. Cool slightly, add the dry red chilli flakes and the salt.
3. Allow to stand for atleast 6 hours before using.

For the cutlets
1. Lightly crush the corn in a mixer.
2. Add the red curry paste, soya sauce, rice flour and salt and mix lightly to make a soft dough.
3. Using lightly greased hands, shape into small flat cutlets of 62 mm. (2½ ") diameter using the mixture and deep-fry in hot oil till they are golden brown.
   Drain on absorbent paper and serve hot with hot and sweet dip.

🌽 *Cheese Corn Balls* 🌽

Corn is an all-time favourite, so is cheese. Put these two together in the form of a crunchy yet soft-centred deep-fried dish, and you have a chartbuster.

Preparation time: 10 minutes.   Cooking time: 20 minutes.   Makes 16 balls.

¾ cup cooked sweet corn kernels (*makai ke dane*), crushed coarsely
1 tbsp plain flour *(maida)*
½ cup milk
1 tbsp chopped celery
1 tsp chopped green chillies
3 to 4 tbsp grated cheese
2 tbsp butter
Salt to taste

For the coating
¼ cup plain flour *(maida)*
Bread crumbs

Other ingredients
Oil for deep-frying

1. Heat the butter in a pan, add the flour and sauté for a minute.
2. Add the milk and keep stirring till the mixture becomes very thick. Cool completely.
3. Add the corn, celery, green chillies, cheese and salt and mix well.
4. Divide the mixture into 16 equal portions and shape them into even sized balls.
5. Mix ¼ cup of flour with water to make a thin paste. Dip the corn balls into the paste.
6. Roll into the breadcrumbs in such a way that they coat the corn balls completely. Chill for 20 minutes. Keep aside.
7. Heat the oil in a *kadhai* and deep-fry the balls in it till they are golden brown.
8. Drain on absorbent paper and serve immediately.

Handy tip : The balls can be made before hand and can be stored for upto 2-3 weeks in the freezer. Follow till step 6, transfer balls in plastic container and store. Defrost and deep-fry in hot oil when you want to serve them.

Baby Corn Fritters

Whip up a desi delight with the hugely popular baby corn. Baby corn marinated in buttermilk and deep fried a perfect start to a meal.

Preparation time: 5 minutes.   Cooking time: 15 minutes.   Makes 32 fritters.

16 nos. baby corn
2 tsp cumin seed (*jeera*) powder
½ tsp rock salt (*sanchal*)
1 cup buttermilk
¼ cup plain flour (*maida*)
½ cup cornflour
Salt to taste

Other ingredients
Oil for deep-frying

For serving
Chilli sauce

1. Make a marinade by mixing together 1 tsp cumin seed powder, rock salt, buttermilk and salt. Keep aside.
2. Wash and slice each baby corn into 2 pieces vertically.
3. Marinate them in the marinade for at least 3 hours.
4. Meanwhile, mix together the plain flour, cornflour, the remaining cumin seed powder and salt with enough water to get a batter of coating consistency.
5. Heat the oil in a *kadhai*, dip the baby corn pieces in the tempura batter and deep-fry till golden brown and crisp. Drain on absorbent paper.
6. Serve hot with chilli sauce.

Handy Tip: You can use *jeeralu* powder instead of the cumin seed powder and rock salt for a unique flavour.

❧ *Stuffed Potato Skins* ❧

Picture on facing page.

Crispy potato cups stuffed with mushrooms and sweet corn. Now, doesn't that sound like heaven? Use small potatoes, and this is an ideal cocktail accompaniment.

Preparation time: 15 minutes.   Cooking time: 20 minutes.   Makes 8.
Baking temperature : 200°C (400°F).   Baking time : 10 minutes.

For the potato skins
8 medium sized potatoes
Salt and pepper to taste
Oil for deep-frying

For the corn filling
1½ cups cooked sweet corn kernels *(makai ke dane)*
¼ cup chopped onions
1 tsp chopped green chillies
¼ cup milk
2 tbsp fresh cream

STUFFED POTATO SKINS : Recipe above. ↪

18

2 tsp cornflour
2 tbsp grated cheese
A few drops Tabasco sauce
2 tbsp butter
Salt to taste

Other ingredients
Grated cooking cheese for baking

For the potato skins
1. Boil the potatoes. Cut them into half lengthwise and scoop out the centre portion leaving fairly thick walls.
2. Deep-fry the potatoes in hot oil until crisp or light pink in colour.
3. Sprinkle salt and pepper over them and keep aside on absorbent paper.

For the corn filling
1. Heat the butter in a pan, add the onions and sauté till they turn translucent.
2. Add the green chillies and corn and sauté again for 2 minutes.
3. Mix the milk, cream, cornflour and salt and add to the mixture. Cook again for a few minutes.

4. Remove from the flame, add the salt, cheese and Tabasco sauce. Mix well and keep aside.

How to proceed
1. Stuff the corn filling in the fried potato skins.
2. Sprinkle some cheese on top and bake in a pre-heated oven at 200°C (400°F) for about 5 minutes or till the cheese melts.
   Serve hot.

🌿 *Corn, Spinach and Rice Balls* 🌿

Bring out the ketchup bottle. Corn, spinach and rice come together in this crunchy, tasty and wholesome snack.

Preparation time: 10 minutes.   Cooking time: 15 minutes.   Makes 12 balls.

1 cup cooked rice
½ cup cooked corn kernels (*makai ke dane*)
½ cup boiled and finely chopped spinach (*palak*)
1 tsp chopped green chillies
Salt to taste

For the sauce
½ cups milk
½ tbsp plain flour (*maida*)
1 tbsp butter

Other ingredients
Rice flour for coating

Oil for deep-frying

For serving
Tomato ketchup

For the sauce
1. Heat the butter in a pan, add the flour and sauté for 1 minute.
2. Add the milk and keep stirring till the sauce is thick. Remove from the flame and keep aside.

How to proceed
1. Add the rice, corn, spinach, green chillies and salt to the sauce and mix well.
2. Divide the mixture into 12 equal sized balls and roll them in rice flour. Keep aside.
3. Heat the oil in a *kadhai* and fry the balls in it till they are golden brown in colour. Drain on absorbent paper and serve hot with tomato ketchup.

🌽 *Spicy Baby Corn* 🌽

Here is an interesting dish made by marinating baby corn in a tempting blend of spices.

Preparation time: 10 minutes.   Cooking time: 10 minutes.   Serves 4.

16 nos. baby corn
2 tbsp oil

To be mixed into a marinade
2 tsp chilli powder
1 tsp grated garlic
¼ tsp carom seeds (*ajwain*)
1 tsp oil
1 tsp cornflour
Salt to taste

For the spring onion and curd dip
¼ cup finely chopped spring onion whites
¼ cup finely chopped spring onion greens

2 stalks celery, roughly chopped
1 clove garlic, finely chopped
1 cup hung curds (*dahi*)
1 tbsp fresh cream (optional)
Salt to taste

For serving
½ cup chopped spring onions
Lemon wedges

For the spring onion and curd dip
1. Combine all the ingredients and blend in a mixer for ½ a minute.
2. Refrigerate to chill.

How to proceed
1. Slit the baby corn into 2 lengthwise.
2. Combine the marinade with the baby corn pieces and 2 to 3 tbsp of water and keep aside for 15 to 20 minutes.
3. Heat the oil in a pan and cook the marinated baby corn over a low flame till they are almost cooked and the marinade has coated the corn.
4. Arrange on a bed of spring onions and lemon wedges and serve with the spring onion and curd dip.

❦ *Crispy Corn Cups* ❦

A sumptuous bread delight! Vitamin A, calcium, crispness, good looks, better taste what else could a connoisseur possibly wish for?

Preparation time: 15 minutes.   Cooking time: 10 minutes.   Makes 8 cups.
Baking temperature : 200°C (400°F).   Baking time : 15 to 20 minutes.

For the toast cases
8 fresh bread slices
Melted butter for greasing and brushing

For the filling
1½ cups cooked corn kernels (*makai ke dane*)
2 tbsp chopped onions
2 tbsp chopped capsicum
2 tsp finely chopped green chillies
1 cup milk
1 tbsp cornflour, dissolved in 2 tbsp of water

1 tbsp oil
Salt to taste

For baking
4 tbsp grated cheese

For the toast cases
1. Remove the crust from the bread slices.
2. Roll out a little with a rolling pin and press into the cavities of a muffin tray which is greased with butter.
3. Brush with melted butter and bake in a hot oven at 200°C (400°F) for 10 minutes or until crisp.

For the filling
1. Heat the oil in a non-stick pan, add the onions and sauté till they are golden brown.
2. Add the capsicum and green chillies and fry for a minute.
3. Add the corn, milk, cornflour and salt and cook till the mixture thickens. Keep aside.

How to proceed
Fill a little mixture in each toast case, sprinkle cheese on top. Bake in hot oven at 200°C (400°F) for 5 to 10 minutes or until the cheese melts.
Serve hot.

Corn Chowder

A typical American thick soup, made more interesting by the pleasant tang of celery...this is a food lover's delight.

Preparation time: 5 minutes.   Cooking time: 15 minutes.   Serves 4.

1 cup cooked sweet corn kernels (*makai ke dane*)
¼ cup chopped onions
2 tbsp chopped celery
3 tbsp plain flour (*maida*)
1 cup milk
1 tbsp butter
Nutmeg (*jaiphal*) powder to taste
Salt and freshly ground pepper to taste

For the garnish
2 tsp grated cheese
1 tbsp chopped celery

1. Grind the corn coarsely in a mixer with 2 cups of water.
2. Heat the butter in a pan, add the onions and celery and sauté till the onions are translucent.
3. Stir in the flour and remove from the flame. Add the milk gradually, while stirring continuously.
4. Return to the flame, add 3 cups of water and simmer gently for 5 minutes.
5. Add the corn, nutmeg powder, salt and pepper and simmer for another 10 minutes.
   Serve hot garnished with cheese and celery.

Nacho Soup

Mexico, here we come! A tasty tomato-based soup, which is topped with corn chips and cheese.

Preparation time: 15 minutes.   Cooking time: 20 minutes.   Serves 4.

½ cup cooked sweet corn kernels (*makai ke dane*)
2 cups nachos, refer handy tip
5 big ripe tomatoes, cut into quarters
¼ cup chopped onions
2 tbsp cornflour
¼ cup grated *paneer* (cottage cheese)
½ vegetarian seasoning cube
½ tsp sugar
2 tbsp butter
Salt to taste

For the garnish
2 tbsp cooked sweet corn kernels (*makai ke dane*)
2 tbsp grated cheese

1. In a pan, add 4 cups of water and tomatoes. Cook till the tomatoes are tender.
2. Blend in a mixer till smooth and pass through a sieve. Keep aside.
3. Heat the butter in a pan, add the onions and sauté till they turn translucent.
4. Mix the cornflour in ½ cup of water.
5. Add the cornflour mixture and tomato purée to the pan and bring to a boil.
6. Add the *paneer*, corn, seasoning cube, sugar and salt and cook for a few minutes.
7. Just before serving, add the nochos and top with corn and cheese.
   Serve hot.

Handy tip : Nachos are deep fried maize flour triangles that are readily available in the market under various brand names.

🌽 *Sweet Corn Soup* 🌽

You can never tire of sweet corn soup. An all-time favourite that is nutritious, tasty, and easy-to-make as well, this is a creamy winner!

Preparation time: 10 minutes.   Cooking time: 5 minutes.   Serves 6.

1 can (450 gms) cream style corn
½ tsp soya sauce
2 tbsp cornflour, dissolved in ¼ cup of water
Salt to taste

To serve
Green chillies in vinegar
Chilli sauce
Soya sauce

1. Mix all the ingredients with 3 cups of water and bring to a boil.
2. Serve hot with chillies in vinegar, chilli sauce and soya sauce.

Handy tips : 1. Always keep a few cans of cream style corn handy so that you can make corn soup and other snacks in a few minutes.
2. Add ½ cup finely chopped vegetables like carrots, french beans, capsicum to make vegetable sweet corn soup.
3. To make chillies in vinegar, thinly slice the green chillies and soak them in vinegar with salt for about 1 hour. This can also be bottled and kept refrigerated for a month.

🌾 *Green Pea Corn Soup* 🌾

Picture on cover.

Green peas and sweet corn ever tried bring the twain together? Cook, blend, and lace with coriander and mint, and the result is a delectable soup that is sure to tease your taste buds.

Preparation time: 15 minutes.   Cooking time: 15 minutes.   Serves 4.

1½ cups green peas
1½ cups sweet corn kernels (*makai ke dane*)
¼ cup chopped onions
1 clove garlic, crushed
¼ cup milk
1 tsp chopped coriander
1 tsp chopped mint (*phudina*)
2 tsp oil
Salt to taste

For the garnish
A few boiled green peas
A few boiled sweet corn kernels (*makai ke dane*)
A few sprigs of mint (*phudina*)

1. Combine the peas, corn, onion, garlic, salt and 4 cups of water and simmer for 10 minutes or until tender.
2. Cool and blend in a mixer to get a smooth purée.
3. Just before serving, add the milk, coriander, mint and salt and bring to a boil. Serve hot garnished with peas, corn and mint.

🌿 *Corn, Basil and Fusilli Soup* 🌿

Viva Italy! This delicately flavoured soup fits perfectly with the finesse of a quiet, home-cooked meal relished with close friends and family.

Preparation time: 5 minutes.   Cooking time: 10 minutes.   Serves 4.

¾ cup boiled fusilli
¾ cup cooked sweet corn kernels (*makai ke dane*)
10 basil leaves, chopped
½ cup chopped onions
2 cloves chopped garlic
1 tsp readymade Pesto sauce, refer handy tip
1 tsp olive oil or oil
Salt and pepper to taste

For the garnish
2 tbsp grated cheese
Basil leaves (optional)

BABY CORN & MUSHROOM SALAD : Recipe on page 46. ➜

1. Heat the oil in a pan, add the onions and garlic and sauté till the onions turn translucent.
2. Add the corn and sauté for a minute.
3. Add 3 cups of water, basil and fusilli and simmer till the fusilli is cooked.
4. Add the pesto, salt and pepper and bring to a boil.
   Serve hot garnished with the cheese and basil leaves.

Handy tip : Pesto is a traditional Italian sauce which is used to flavour various soups and pastas. It can be made by blending together 2 tbsp of basil leaves, 1 tbsp of pine nuts and 1 tbsp of olive oil in a mixer.

Spinach and Baby Corn Soup

Coconut milk powder is the magic ingredient that makes this soup unique and unbelievably tasty.

Preparation time: 10 minutes.   Cooking time: 10 minutes.   Serves 4.

1½ cups chopped spinach (*palak*)
½ cup sliced baby corn
2 cloves chopped garlic
2 chopped spring onions
4 tsp coconut milk powder
1 tsp butter
Salt to taste

1. Boil 2 cups of water.
2. Meanwhile, heat the butter in a saucepan and sauté the garlic and spring onions in it for a couple of minutes.
3. Add the spinach and baby corn and sauté for a few more minutes.
4. Sprinkle the coconut milk powder and stir well.
5. Add the hot water and salt and simmer till the baby corns are cooked. Serve hot.

🌾 *Makai Shorba* 🌾

This luscious and luxurious Indian-style corn soup is sure to steal everybody's heart. Served hot with garlic bread, it makes an absolutely healthy, hearty and wholesome meal.

Preparation time: 5 minutes.   Cooking time: 15 minutes.   Serves 2.

1½ cups sweet corn kernels (*makai ke dane*)
2 cloves (*laung / lavang*)
25 mm. (1") stick cinnamon (*dalchini*)
3-4 peppercorns
1 bay leaf (*tejpatta*)
½ cup chopped onions
4 cloves garlic, sliced
½ cup carrot cubes
1 tsp crushed coriander (*dhania*) seeds
½ tsp cumin seeds (*jeera*) powder
A pinch turmeric powder (*haldi*)
2 cups milk
2 tsp oil

Salt to taste

For the garnish
Roasted sweet corn kernels (*makai ke dane*)
Sprig of coriander

For serving
Lemon juice

1. Heat the oil in a non-stick pan, add the cloves, cinnamon, peppercorns, bay leaf, onions and garlic and cook till the onions are translucent.
2. Add the carrots, coriander seeds, cumin seeds powder and turmeric powder and cook for 3 to 4 minutes.
3. Add the corn, 3½ cups of water and salt and simmer over a medium flame for 10 to 15 minutes, till the corn is cooked.
4. Cool completely and blend to a smooth purée in a mixer. Transfer back into a pan.
5. Add the milk, bring to a boil garnished with roasted corn and coriander sprig.
6. Serve hot with the lemon juice.

SALADS

Mexican Bean and Cheese Salad

Picture on page 2.

A cold salad of corn tossed together with a variety of interesting ingredients like chawli, rajma and cheese.

Preparation time: 20 minutes.   Cooking time: Nil.   Serves 4.

1 cup cooked sweet corn kernels (*makai ke dane*)
¼ cup boiled *chawli* (black-eyed beans)
1 cup boiled *rajma* (kidney beans)
½ cup chopped tomatoes
½ cup processed cheese cubes
¼ cup chopped spring onion whites
¼ cup chopped spring onion greens
2 tbsp chopped coriander
Salt to taste

42

To be mixed into a dressing (in a bottle)
2 tbsp lemon juice
½ tsp salt
2 pinches sugar
¼ tsp chilli powder
4 tbsp salad oil / oil

For the garnish
Few broken corn chips (optional)

1. Combine the dressing ingredients in a bowl. Transfer to a glass bottle and shake well
2. Mix the corn, *chawli, rajma*, tomato, cheese, spring onion whites, spring onion greens, coriander and salt.
3. Toss in the dressing and keep in a refrigerator.
4. Just before serving, remove from the refrigerator and top with corn chips. Serve immediately.

🌽 *Burnt Corn Salad* 🌽

Grilling fresh corn kernels over an open flame imparts this dish a typically-Mexican barbecued flavour to this light and nutritious salad.

Preparation time: 10 minutes.   Cooking time: 5 minutes.   Serves 4.

1 sweet corn cob (*bhutta*)
½ cup onion slices
¼ cup capsicum slices
¼ cup tomato slices
Salt to taste

To be mixed into a dressing
1 tbsp olive oil
2 tbsp lemon juice
2 pinches chilli powder
Salt to taste

1. Roast the corn cob over an open flame until the corn is slightly burnt. Using a sharp knife, remove the corn kernels (*makai ke dane*) from the cob. Keep aside.
2. Combine the corn, onions, capsicum, tomatoes and salt.
3. Pour the dressing on top and toss well. Serve immediately.

🌽 Baby Corn and Mushroom Salad 🌽

Picture on page 37.

A colourful selection of vegetables dressed with a delicious blend of garlic and basil.

Preparation time: 10 minutes.   Cooking time: 2 minutes.   Serves 4.

½ cup spring onion cubes
½ cup fresh mushroom slices
½ cup blanched and cubed baby corn
¾ cup bean sprouts
½ cup cubed red and green capsicums
½ cup cucumber cubes

For the dressing
1 tbsp olive oil
3 cloves finely chopped garlic
1 tbsp finely chopped fresh basil leaves
2 tsp lemon juice
1 tsp sugar
Salt and pepper to taste

For the dressing
1. Heat the oil in a non-stick pan, add the garlic and sauté till it browns lightly.
2. Add the basil leaves and mix well. Cool completely.
3. Add the lemon juice, sugar, salt and pepper and mix well.

How to proceed
1. Combine all the ingredients in a bowl and toss lightly. Refrigerate.
2. Just before serving, add the dressing to the salad and toss well.
   Serve immediately.

Handy Tip: If you cannot find fresh basil, substitute it with ¼ tsp of dried basil, as
dried herbs have more contentrated flavours than fresh herbs.

🌽 *Chatpata Salad* 🌽

This tangy sweet corn salad is easy to put together and jam-packed with flavour and fun!

Preparation time: 10 minutes.   No cooking.   Serves 6 to 8.

1½ cups cooked sweet corn kernels (*makai ke dane*)
2 boiled potatoes, peeled and cut into pieces
½ cup *paneer* (cottage cheese) cubes
2 spring onions, chopped
¾ chopped tomatoes
½ tsp lemon juice
½ tsp finely chopped green chillies
2 tsp *chaat masala*
2 tsp *chunda* (sweet raw mango pickle)
1 tbsp chopped coriander
Salt to taste

1. Mix all the ingredients very well.
2. Store in a refrigerator. Serve chilled.

48

INDIAN CORN DISHES

Baby Corn Hara Masala

Rang bhare baby corn! Chunks of baby corn cooked in a spicy coriander paste, this dish is delightful to see and taste.

Preparation time: 10 minutes.   Cooking time: 10 minutes.   Serves 4.

2 cups baby corn, cut into 4 lengthwise
1 tsp lemon juice
1 tsp sugar
3 tbsp oil
Salt to taste

To be ground into a paste
1½ cups chopped coriander
12 mm. (½") piece ginger

49

2 cloves garlic
2 green chillies
1 cup chopped onions
1 tsp cumin seeds (*jeera*)
½ tsp lemon juice

For the garnish
1 tbsp sliced tomatoes
4 lemon wedges

1. Heat the oil in a pan, add the prepared paste and sauté for 5 minutes.
2. Add the baby corn, salt and 2 tbsp of water and mix well. Cook for 1 minute.
3. Add the lemon juice and sugar. Mix well.
   Serve hot garnished with the tomatoes and lemon wedges.

🌽 *Corn Curry* 🌽

A green curry tinged with coconut and coriander, this will leave your taste buds yearning for more.

Preparation time: 15 minutes.   Cooking time: 10 minutes.   Serves 4.

1½ cups cooked white corn (*makai ke dane*)
2 cups coconut milk
1 tsp cornflour
2 sticks cinnamon (*dalchini*)
2 cloves (*laung / lavang*)
2 cardamoms (*elaichi*)
Juice of ½ lemon
2 tbsp oil
Salt to taste

To be ground into a paste
1½ cups chopped coriander
½ cup sliced onions
2 green chillies

51

2 tbsp freshly grated coconut
5 cloves garlic
4 tsp poppy seeds (*khus-khus*)
12 mm. (½″) piece ginger

For serving
Steamed rice

1. Dissolve the cornflour in the coconut milk and keep aside.
2. Heat the oil in a pan and fry the prepared paste for 5 minutes.
3. Add the cinnamon, cloves and cardamoms and fry again for a minute.
4. Add the lemon juice and mix well.
5. Add the corn, coconut milk, ½ cup of water and salt. Mix well and cook for a few minutes.

   Serve hot with steamed rice.

❧ *Makai Paatal Bhaji* ❧

Picture on page 55.

A unique sweet and spicy blend of colocasia leaves, chana dal and spices forms the base for this Maharashtrian-style dish made with hearty chunks of corn on the cob.

Preparation time: 20 minutes.   Cooking time: 30 minutes.   Serves 4.

2 sweet corncobs (*bhutta*), cut into 25 mm. (1") pieces, boiled
½ tsp cumin seeds (*jeera*)
½ tsp asafoetida (*hing*)
½ tsp grated ginger
1 tsp chopped green chillies
4 cups finely chopped colocassia (*arbi*) leaves
½ cup boiled *chana dal* (split Bengal gram)
¼ tsp turmeric powder (*haldi*)
½ tsp coriandercumin seed (*dhania-jeera*) powder
2 tsp tamarind (*imli*) pulp
1 tbsp grated jaggery (*gur*)
Salt to taste

1. Heat the oil in a pan, add the cumin seeds, asafoetida, ginger and green chillies.
2. Add the colocasia leaves, *chana dal*, turmeric powder, coriander-cumin seed powder and salt and sauté till the mixture comes together as a mass.
3. Add 1 cup of water and pressure cook for 3 whistles.
4. Whisk well till it is smooth.
5. Add the corncobs, tamarind pulp and jaggery and bring to a boil.
    Serve hot.

MAKAI PAATAL BHAJI : Recipe on page 53. ↪

Methi Makai

Sweet corn kernels heartily coated with a thick gravy, rich in the goodness of methi.

Preparation time: 10 minutes.   Cooking time: 15 minutes.   Serves 4.

2 cups cooked sweet corn kernels (*makai ke dane*)
¾ cup onion slices
2 cloves garlic, roughly chopped
12 mm. (½") piece ginger, chopped
2 green chillies, chopped
2 tbsp chopped cashewnuts (*kaju*)
1 cup milk
½ cup fresh thick curds (*dahi*)
2 tsp *besan* (Bengal gram flour)
¼ tsp turmeric powder (*haldi*)
½ tsp cumin seeds (*jeera*)
¾ cup chopped fenugreek (*methi*) leaves
1 tsp coriander (*dhania*) powder
¼ cup cream

2 tbsp oil
Salt to taste

1. Boil the onions, garlic, ginger, green chillies and cashewnuts with the milk for about 10 to 15 minutes.
2. Cool and blend in a mixer to get a smooth purée. Keep aside.
3. Whisk the curds, *besan* and turmeric powder till smooth and keep aside.
4. Heat the oil in a pan and add the cumin seeds.
5. When they crackle, add the fenugreek leaves and coriander powder and sauté for about 3 to 4 minutes.
6. Add the onion purée, curds-*besan* mixture, corn and salt and simmer for some time till the gravy thickens and coats the corn.
7. Add the cream and stir for 1 to 2 minutes.
   Serve hot.

❦ *Palak Baby Corn* ❧

The versatile palak, a favourite in North Indian households, can be used in a variety of preparations such as raita, soup, gravy and kofta! Here it combines with corn, to delight your senses.

Preparation time: 15 minutes.   Cooking time: 25 minutes.   Serves 4.

16 baby corn, cut into 25 mm. (1") pieces and boiled
1 cup spinach (*palak*) purée, refer handy tip
¾ tsp chopped garlic
1 tsp grated ginger
1 tsp dried fenugreek leaves (*kasuri methi*)
¾ tsp *garam masala*
1 tsp sugar
¼ cup cream
¼ cup finely chopped tomatoes
½ tsp black salt
2 tbsp oil
1 tbsp butter
Salt to taste

For the white gravy
1 cup sliced onions
10 cashewnuts (*kaju*)
2 tbsp melon seeds (*charmagaz*)
3 green chillies

For the white gravy
1. Combine all the ingredients with 1½ cups of water and simmer for about 15 minutes.
2. Cool and blend to a smooth paste in a mixer. Keep aside.

How to proceed
1. Heat the oil and butter in a pan and add the ginger, garlic and tomatoes to it.
2. Sauté for sometime and then add the white gravy, spinach purée, black salt and salt. Cook till oil separates from the gravy.
3. Add the baby corn, dried fenugreek leaves, garam masala, sugar and cream and bring to a boil. Serve hot.

Handy tip: To make spinach purée, clean the spinach leaves, blanch them in hot water, drain and grind. About 1 cup spinach leaves gives ¼ cup of purée.

❧ *Palak Makai Khaas* ❧

In this luxurious Hyderabadi-recipe, an aromatic gravy of spinach spiked with roasted coconut adds a unique flavour to the sweet corn kernels. Serve with fresh hot parathas for a perfect North meets South combination.

Preparation time: 10 minutes.   Cooking time: 25 minutes.   Serves 4.

1½ cups cooked sweet corn kernels (*makai ke dane*)
4 cups spinach (*palak*) leaves
1 tsp cumin seeds (*jeera*)
¼ tsp asafoetida (*hing*)
½ cup finely chopped onions
1½ tsp ginger-green chilli paste
1 tsp *kasuri methi* (dried fenugreek leaves)
3 tbsp desiccated coconut
½ tsp roasted cumin seeds (*jeera*) powder
2 tbsp oil
Salt to taste

1. Blanch the spinach in boiling water for 2 to 3 minutes. Drain and pour cold water to refresh the spinach. Drain again.
2. Blend the spinach in a mixer to a smooth purée. Keep aside.
3. Heat the oil in a pan, add the cumin seeds and asafoetida.
4. When the seeds crackle, add the onions and ginger-green chilli paste and sauté till the onions turn translucent.
5. Add the *kasuri methi* and desiccated coconut and sauté till the coconut is lightly browned and crisp (approx. 4 to 5 minutes).
6. Add the puréed spinach, corn, roasted cumin seed powder and salt and mix well. Serve hot.

❦ *Corn Pulao* ❦

What would a meal be without a rice dish! This baked pulao is loaded with yummy sweet corn kernels, and is undoubtedly a favourite with young and old alike.

Preparation time: 15 minutes.   Cooking time: 15 minutes.   Serves 4.
Baking time : 15 minutes.   Baking temperature : 200°C (400°F).

For the rice
2½ cups cooked long grain rice
½ cup milk
1 tbsp butter
Salt to taste

For the corn layer
1½ cup of cooked tender sweet corn kernels (*makai ke dane*)
½ tsp cumin seeds (*jeera*)
½ cup chopped onion
½ tsp chopped green chillies
1 tbsp oil

Salt to taste

Other ingredients
Oil or butter for greasing

For serving
Kadhi of your choice

For the rice
Heat the butter in a pan on a slow flame and add the rice, milk and salt. Cook for 1 minute and keep aside.

For the corn layer
1. Heat the oil in a pan and add the cumin seeds.
2. When they crackle, add the onions and fry for a minute.
3. Add the green chillies and fry again for a few seconds.
4. Add the corn and salt and cook till the corn is done.

How to proceed
1. Spread the corn mixture at the bottom of a greased jelly mould.
2. Spread the rice on top. Press well and cover with an aluminium foil.
3. Bake in a pre-heated oven at 200°C (400°F) for 10 minutes.
4. While serving, invert on a plate and serve hot with a kadhi of your choice.

INTERNATIONAL CORN DISHES

Baby Corn and Soya Stir-fry

Picture on facing page.

When it comes to health food, stir-fries are always on top of my list, as it is quite easy to monitor the amount of fat used. I have chosen soya nuggets because of their low 'bad' cholesterol, and baby corn adds the much-needed crunch without adding to the fat as well.

Preparation time: 15 minutes. Cooking time: 10 minutes. Serves 4.

1 cup parboiled baby corn, cut into 25 mm (1″) pieces
½ cup soya nuggets
2 tsp chopped garlic
¼ cup chopped spring onion whites
½ cup capsicum cubes
¾ cup sliced mushrooms

BABY CORN AND SOYA STIR-FRY : Recipe above. →

3 tsp soya sauce
2 tbsp tomato-chilli sauce
½ cup chopped spring onion greens
1 tbsp oil
A pinch sugar
Salt to taste

1. Soak the soya nuggets in warm water for 10 to 15 minutes. Drain and squeeze out all the water.
2. Heat the oil in a non-stick pan, add the garlic, spring onion whites and capsicum and sauté over high flame till the onions turn golden brown in colour.
3. Add the mushrooms and sauté for 1 minute.
4. Add the soya nuggets and baby corn and sauté for 2 minutes.
5. Add the soya sauce, tomato-chilli sauce, sugar and salt and cook for 2 more minutes.
6. Add the spring onion greens and cook for another minute.
   Serve immediately.

Baked Corn Sandwich

A simple sandwich transforms into a delicacy, thanks to the magic of corn.

Preparation time: 10 minutes.   Cooking time: 10 minutes.   Serves 4.
Baking time : 25 minutes.   Baking temperature : 220°C (440°F).

8 bread slices
1 cup cooked white corn kernels
(*makai ke dane*)
½ cup chopped onions
2 tsp chopped green chillies
2 pinches sugar
1 cup milk
4 tbsp grated cooking cheese
1 tbsp butter
Salt and pepper to taste

For the white sauce
1 tbsp butter
1 tbsp plain flour (*maida*)
1 cup milk
Salt and freshly ground
pepper to taste

For the white sauce
1. Melt the butter in a pan and add the flour.
2. Cook the flour on a slow flame while stirring continuously.
3. Add the milk gradually and stir continuously until the sauce thickens.
4. Add salt and pepper and mix well. Keep aside.

How to proceed
1. Melt the butter in a pan, add the onions and green chillies and sauté for 1 minute.
2. Add the corn, sugar, salt and ½ cup of white sauce. Cook for 1 minute, remove and keep aside.
3. Cut and discard the crust from the bread slices. Dip them in the milk.
4. Arrange 4 bread slices on a greased rectangular baking dish.
5. Layer half of the corn mixture on the slices and top with the remaining 4 bread slices. Again layer the remaining corn mixture.
6. Dissolve a little of salt in the remaining milk and pour on top.
7. Add the pepper and half of the cheese to the remaining white sauce. Spread over the sandwiches.
8. Top with the remaining cheese and bake in a pre-heated oven at 220°C (440°F) for 20 minutes.
   Cut into triangles and serve hot.

🌽 *Corn Manchurian* 🌽

Forget mundane things like the weighing scale and dig into these deep fried vegetable balls dipped in soya sauce based gravy! This ever popular Chinese dish is also really easy to make.

Preparation time: 15 minutes.   Cooking time: 20 minutes.   Serves 4.

For the corn balls
2 cups grated corn kernels (*makai ke dane*)
¼ cups grated carrots
¼ cup chopped onions
2 tbsp cornflour
5 tbsp plain flour (*maida*)
1 tsp finely chopped garlic
1 tsp finely chopped green chillies
¼ tsp Mono sodium glutamate (MSG), optional
Salt and pepper to taste

For the sauce
1 tbsp finely chopped garlic

2 tsp finely chopped green chillies
2 tsp finely chopped ginger
1½ cups clear vegetable stock or water
1 tbsp soya sauce
2 tbsp cornflour mixed with 1 cup water
2 pinches sugar
2 tbsp oil
Salt to taste

Other ingredients
Oil for deep-frying

For the corn balls

1. Mix the corn, carrots, onions, cornflour, plain flour, garlic, green chillies, MSG, salt and pepper.
2. Shape spoonfuls of the mixture into small balls. If you find it difficult to form balls, sprinkle a little water to bind the mixture.
3. Heat the oil in a wok and deep-fry the balls in hot oil until golden brown. Drain on absorbent paper and keep aside.

For the sauce

1. Heat the oil in a wok or frying pan on a high flame. Add the garlic, green chillies and ginger and stir-fry over a high flame for a few seconds.
2. Add the stock, soya sauce, cornflour paste, sugar and salt and simmer for a few minutes.

How to serve

Just before serving, put the corn balls in the sauce and bring to a boil. Serve hot.

Handy tip : To make vegetable stock, just add the vegetables like carrots, spring onions, capsicum and white pumpkin to a vesselful of water and simmer for about 20 minutes. Strain, use the liquid as stock and discard the vegetables.

🌿 *Steamed Curry Rice* 🌿

Coconut milk, sliced baby corn and basil add a really exquisite flavour to this rice dish.
You must taste it to believe the heavenly experience.

Preparation time: 15 minutes.   Cooking time: 25 minutes.   Serves 4.

3 cups cooked long grained rice
¾ cup coconut milk
½ tsp cornflour
2 tbsp garlic paste
1 tbsp red chilli paste
¼ cup French beans, sliced diagonally and boiled
¼ cup boiled green peas
¼ cup boiled and sliced baby corn
1 tbsp finely chopped fresh basil
1 tsp lemon rind
2 tbsp olive oil/oil
Salt to taste

Other ingredients
1 banana leaf

1. Dissolve the cornflour in the coconut milk. Keep aside.
2. Heat the oil in a pan, add the garlic paste and red chilli paste and cook for 3 to 4 minutes.
3. Add the coconut milk mixture, all the boiled vegetables, basil, lemon rind and salt and cook for a couple of more minutes so the mixture thickens.
4. Add the rice and mix well.
5. Turn this flavoured rice onto the centre of a banana leaf (kitchen foil can be used as substitute).
6. Fold the leaf into a square packet and steam in a steamer till done.

Handy tip: Red chilli paste is made by soaking dry red chillies in lukewarm water for about 15 minutes and then grinding with little water to a smooth paste.

❧ *Oriental Rice Noodles* ❧

Picture on page 75.

A typical example of an on-the-go snack, this recipe is the best way to keep your little ones' hunger pangs satiated.

Preparation time: 15 minutes.   Cooking time: 10 minutes.   Serves 4.

3 cups cooked rice noodles
2 tbsp oil

For the chilli paneer and baby corn mixture
½ cup *paneer* (cottage cheese), cut into 12 mm. (½") cubes
1 cup baby corn, boiled and cut into 25 mm. (1") pieces
¼ cup chopped spring onion whites
½ tsp chopped celery
2 tsp finely chopped green chillies
½ tsp chopped garlic
½ tsp chopped ginger
¼ cup chopped capsicum
½ cup finely chopped spring onion greens

2 tsp oil

To be mixed together into a soya sauce mixture
1 tsp soya sauce
1 tsp cornflour
½ tsp sugar
Salt to taste
Pepper to taste
¼ cup water

For the chilli paneer and baby corn mixture
1. Heat the oil in a non-stick pan, add the spring onion whites and sauté for 2 minutes, till the onions turn translucent.
2. Add the celery, green chillies, garlic and ginger and cook for another minute.
3. Add the capsicum, *paneer*, baby corn and the prepared soya sauce mixture and cook for 2 more minutes, till the sauce thickens and coats the vegetables and *paneer*.
4. Add the spring onion greens and mix well. Keep aside.

How to proceed
1. Heat the oil in a wok and add the chilli *paneer* and baby corn mixture.
2. Add the rice noodles and toss well. Serve hot.

Handy tip : To cook rice noodles, soak them in boiling hot water for 10 to 15 minutes or as the instruction on the package specify. Drain the water and again put in cold water in order to arrest any further cooking. Drain and use as required.

ORIENTAL RICE NOODLES : Recipe on page 73. ↪

Creamy Corn Pizza

Presto, here we have a creamy pesto-flavoured corn sauce, topped with roasted coloured capsicum.
Sure to delight all those who taste it!

Preparation time: 15 minutes.   Cooking time: 5 minutes.   Makes 2 pizzas.
Baking temperature : 200°C (400°F).   Baking time : 30 minutes.

2 pizza bases, 200 mm. (8") diameter
1 red capsicum
1 green capsicum
1 yellow capsicum
2 tbsp tomato ketchup
1 tbsp tomato chilli sauce
1 cup grated mozzarella cheese
Butter or oil for greasing
Salt to taste

To be mixed into a corn pesto mixture
1 cup cream style sweet corn (canned)
3 tbsp pesto, refer handy tip
Salt to taste

1. Pierce a fork into each capsicum, grease them with oil and roast on an open flame till it is chared.
2. Remove, cut into thin slices and wash thoroughly. Keep aside.
3. Place one pizza base on a greased baking tray.
4. Spread 1 tbsp tomato ketchup and ½ tbsp tomato chilli sauce on it.
5. Spread half the corn pesto mixture and half the capsicum slices over it.
6. Sprinkle a little salt and then spread half the cheese on top.
7. Bake in a preheated oven at 200°C (400°F) for 10 minutes or till the base is evenly browned and the cheese melts.
8. Repeat with the remaining ingredients to make another pizza.
   Serve hot.

Handy tip : Pesto is a traditional Italian sauce which is used to flavour various soups and pastas. It can be made by blending together 2 tbsp of basil leaves, 1 tbsp of pine nuts and 1 tbsp of olive oil in a mixer.

Farfel with Baby Corn and Walnuts

Picture on page 85.

Farfel is a variety of pasta that is shaped like a butterfly. It is usually served with a spicy tomato sauce. Here, you see an unusual combination of farfel tossed with baby corn, walnuts and a sprinkling of fresh basil and parsley.

Preparation time: 10 minutes.   Cooking time: 10 minutes.   Serves 4.

3 cups cooked farfel
¼ cup finely chopped onions
2 tsp finely chopped garlic
¼ cup finely chopped walnuts
1 cup sliced baby corn
2 tbsp finely chopped parsley
2 tbsp finely chopped fresh basil
A pinch nutmeg (*jaiphal*)
4 tbsp olive oil or butter
Salt and freshly ground pepper to taste

78

For serving
3 tbsp grated Parmesan cheese or processed cheese

1. Heat the olive oil in a pan, add the onions and garlic and sauté till the onions turn translucent.
2. Add the walnuts and baby corn and sauté for 3 to 4 minutes so the baby corn is cooked.
3. Add the farfel, parsley, basil, nutmeg, salt and pepper and toss well.
   Serve hot garnished with cheese.

Chinese Vegetables in Hot Garlic Sauce

Chinese cooking is almost synonymous with hot garlic sauce. Here, the sauce joins hands with baby corn and other interesting vegetables to provide an enjoyable dining experience.

Preparation time: 10 minutes.   Cooking time: 10 minutes.   Serves 4.

1 cup cauliflower florets, parboiled
½ cup sliced capsicum
½ cup sliced baby corn, parboiled
¼ cup sliced french beans, parboiled
2 tsp finely chopped ginger
2 tsp finely chopped garlic
2 tsp finely chopped green chillies
¼ cup tomato purée
2 tsp cornflour mixed with 1 cup of water
A pinch sugar (optional)
2 tbsp oil
Salt to taste

1. Heat the oil in a wok of frying pan on a high flame. Add the ginger, garlic and green chillies and stir-fry over a high flame for a few seconds.
2. Add the vegetables and sauté for a few minutes.
3. Add the tomato purée, cornflour paste, sugar and salt and simmer for a few minutes.
   Serve hot.

DAY-TO-DAY CORN SNACKS

❧ *Cheesy Corn Rawa Waffles* ❧

Crispy rawa waffles topped with corn, cheese and tomatoes! A tongue-tickling snack, this is best eaten as soon as it is made. And remember to add the fruit salt just before you are ready to cook the waffles.

Preparation time: 5 minutes.   Cooking time: 10 minutes.   Makes 4 waffles.

1 cup semolina (*rawa*)
¾ cup *urad dal* (split black lentil) flour
1½ tbsp fresh thick curds (*dahi*)
1 tsp finely chopped green chillies
½ tsp crushed cumin seeds (*jeera*)
¼ tsp asafoetida (*hing*)
2 tbsp chopped coriander
1 tsp fruit salt
1½ tbsp oil
Salt to taste

To be mixed into a topping

¾ cup cooked white corn kernels (*makai ke dane*)
½ cup finely chopped capsicum
¼ cup finely chopped tomatoes
½ cup grated mozzarella cheese or cooking cheese

Other ingredients

Oil for cooking

1. Combine the semolina, *urad dal* flour, curds, green chillies, cumin seeds, asafoetida, coriander, oil, salt and approx. 1 cup of water. Mix well to get a smooth batter.
2. Add the fruit salt and mix gently.
3. Pre-heat a waffle iron.
4. Lightly grease the waffle iron with some oil, pour ¼ of the waffle batter and spread evenly. Cook for 2 minutes or until the waffle is golden brown.
5. Put ¼ of the topping mixture on the waffle and warm it up in an open waffle iron for 1 to 2 minutes or until the cheese has melted.
6. Repeat with the remaining batter and ingredients to make 3 more waffles. Serve hot.

✹ *Makai ni Khichdi* ✹

The traditional khichdi takes on a completely new avatar when made with grated white corn.

Preparation time: 15 minutes.   Cooking time: 25 minutes.   Serves 4.

3 cups grated white corn (*makai ke dane*)
½ tsp mustard seeds (*rai / sarson*)
½ tsp cumin seeds (*jeera*)
¼ tsp asafoetida (*hing*)
2 tsp chopped green chillies
½ cup milk
1 tsp sugar
Juice of ½ lemon
2 tbsp oil
Salt to taste

FARFEL WITH BABY CORN AND WALNUTS: Recipe on page 78. ➜

For the garnish
2 tbsp chopped coriander

1. Heat the oil in a pan, add the mustard seeds, cumin seeds, asafoetida and green chillies.
2. When the seeds crackle, add the corn and cook on a slow flame for 5 minutes while stirring continuously.
3. Add the milk, sugar, salt and enough water to cover the corn. Add the sugar and salt.
4. Cover and simmer till the corn is tender.
5. Add the lemon juice and mix well.
   Serve hot garnished with coriander.

🌿 *Corn and Cottage Cheese Tacos* 🌿

Picture on back cover.

Tacos stuffed with corn and paneer and topped with an interesting green sauce, this dish is guaranteed to delight the diners.

Preparation time: 15 minutes. Cooking time: 15 minutes. Serves 4.

12 tacos

For the stuffing
¼ cup chopped onions
1 cup cooked white and yellow corn kernels
(*makai ke dane*)
½ cup *paneer* (cottage cheese), cut into cubes
¼ cup chopped yellow capsicum
¼ cup chopped tomatoes
2 tsp chopped green chillies
2 tbsp oil
Salt to taste

For the green sauce
1 small capsicum, deseeded and
cut into chunks
½ cup milk
1 tbsp butter
2 tbsp plain flour (*maida*)
Salt and freshly ground pepper
to taste

For the topping
6 olives, cut into half
½ cup shredded lettuce leaves

87

For the stuffing
1. Heat the oil in a pan, add the onions and sauté for a few seconds.
2. Add the corn, *paneer*, capsicum, tomatoes, coriander and salt and mix well. Keep aside.

For the green sauce
1. Put the capsicum in boiling water. After a few minutes, remove and blend with the milk in a mixer.
2. Heat the butter in a pan and fry the flour for ½ minutes. Add the blended milk and go on stirring until the sauce thickens.
3. Add salt and pepper. Keep aside.

How to proceed
1. Just before serving, sprinkle some green sauce and put some stuffing in each taco.
2. Top with olives and lettuce and serve immediately.

Satay Sticks

Satay sticks to stimulate your taste buds. Baby corn, paneer and capsicum marinated in lemon juice and honey, toasted as a satay stick, and served with peanut sauce, this is an ideal finger food.

Preparation time: 10 minutes. Cooking time: 8 minutes. Serves 4.

½ cup baby corn, cut into 25 mm. (1") pieces and parboiled
½ cup *paneer* (cottage cheese), cut into 12 mm. (½ ") cubes
½ cup green or red capsicum, cut into 12 mm. (½") cubes
Oil for cooking

To be mixed into a marinade
1 tbsp curry powder
2 tsp lemon juice
2 tsp honey
½ tsp salt
1 tbsp oil

For the peanut sauce
2 tbsp peanut butter
½ tsp soya sauce
1 tsp sugar
½ tsp chilli powder
Salt to taste

For the peanut sauce
1. Combine all the ingredients in a pan with ½ cup of water. Mix well.
2. Bring the sauce to a boil. Remove and keep aside.

How to proceed
1. In a large bowl, combine the baby corn, *paneer*, capsicum and the prepared marinade and toss well.
2. Arrange a piece of baby corn, *paneer* and capsicum on a toothpick.
3. Repeat for the remaining vegetables (to make approx. 15 sticks).
4. Heat little oil on a *tava* (griddle) and sauté the satay sticks on all sides till the vegetables are lightly browned (approx. 4 to 5 minutes).
   Serve hot with peanut sauce.

Corn Sev Puris

Street food enters your kitchen, and in a new corn-rich avatar! Papadis or little puris are topped with sweet corn and crunchy onions, and spiked with a tangy ajwain-flavoured tomato chutney.

Preparation time: 10 minutes.   Cooking time: 15 minutes.   Serves 4.

24 *papadis*
1 recipe tomato *chutney*, recipe below
1 cup nylon *sev* or *sev*
¼ cup fresh pomegranate (*anar*)
2 tbsp chopped coriander

To be mixed together into a corn topping
1 cup cooked sweet corn kernels (*makai ke dane*)
½ cup chopped onions
1 tsp finely chopped green chillies
¼ cup finely chopped tomatoes
1 tsp chaat masala

2 tsp lemon juice
Salt to taste

For the tomato chutney
4 medium sized tomatoes
½ tsp carom seeds (*ajwain*)
A pinch asafoetida (*hing*)
1 tsp grated garlic
½ tsp chilli powder
½ tsp sugar
1 tbsp oil
Salt to taste

For the tomato chutney

1. Blanch the tomatoes in hot water. Peel and blend in a mixer to a smooth purée.
2. Heat the oil in a pan, add the carom seeds and asafoetida and sauté for 10 seconds.
3. Add the garlic and sauté for a few seconds.
4. Add the puréed tomatoes, chilli powder, sugar and salt and bring to a boil.
5. Simmer for 20 minutes or till the oil has separated. Cool and keep aside.

How to proceed

1. Arrange the *papadis* on a serving plate.
2. Top each *papadi* with 2 tsp of the corn topping.
3. Put 1 tsp of the tomato *chutney* on each *papadi* and garnish with the chopped coriander, sev and pomegranate.
   Serve immediately.

🌾 *Pearly Corn* 🌾

Sweet corn kernels, coated in batter and deep fried, is phenomenally interesting when served with a sprinkling of spring onions and tomatoes. These corn titbits look like small pearls, and are a lovely accompaniment for rice or noodles.

Preparation time: 10 minutes.   Cooking time: 15 minutes.   Serves 4.

1 cup sweet corn kernels (*makai ke dane*)
½ cup plain flour (*maida*)
¼ cup cornflour
½ tsp readymade mustard paste
1 tsp chilli powder
½ cup water
Salt and pepper to taste

Other ingredients
Oil for deep-frying

For the garnish
2 tbsp chopped spring onion greens
1 tsp chopped tomatoes (optional)

1. Mix together all the ingredients except the oil in a bowl and keep aside.
2. Heat the oil in a *kadhai* and scatter individual batter coated kernels in the oil.
   Deep-fry until they are golden brown in colour and drain on absorbent paper.
3. Serve immediately, garnished with spring onion greens and tomatoes

Paneer and Corn Burger

This is a perfect no-fuss yet mouth-watering snack for a crowd. All you need are mini burger buns and small patties made with paneer and sweet corn.

Preparation time: 20 minutes.   Cooking time: 15 minutes.   Makes 4 burgers.

4 burger buns
4 tbsp eggless mayonnaise
1 thinly sliced tomatoes
1 thinly sliced onions
½ cup shredded lettuce
Salt and freshly ground pepper to taste

For the filling
½ cup crumbled *paneer* (cottage cheese)
½ cup crushed sweet corn (*makai ke dane*), canned
1 tsp finely chopped green chillies
2 tbsp chopped coriander

2 tbsp bread crumbs
1 tbsp cornflour
Salt to taste
Bread crumbs for coating
Oil for deep-frying

For serving
French fries

95

For the filling

1. Combine all the ingredients in a bowl and mix well. Divide into 4 equal portions.
2. Shape each portion into a patty.
3. Coat the patty with bread crumbs.
4. Heat oil in a *kadhai* and deep-fry the patties till they are golden brown.
5. Drain on absorbent paper and keep aside.

How to proceed

1. Slit each burger bun into 2 halves. Toast both sides of each slit bun lightly on a tava (griddle).
2. Place one patty on the base of a toasted burger bun. Top with 1 tbsp of mayonnaise, some tomato slices, onion slices, shredded lettuce and sprinkle salt and pepper. Sandwich with the other half of the burger bun.
3. Repeat with the remaining ingredients to make 3 more burgers.
   Serve hot with French fries.

Handy tip : Drain out all the juices of the canned sweet corn before using it for the above recipe.

Cheesy Corn Stuffed Jacket Potatoes

A cheese and corn topping that goes just as well with jacket potatoes as it does with bread. This serves as an interesting tea-time snack, and could also serve as a wholesome supper if served with soup and salad.

Preparation time: 5 minutes.   Cooking time: 10 minutes.   Serves 4.
Baking time : 8 to 10 minutes.   Baking temperature : 200°C (400°F).

4 large potatoes, boiled with the skin on
Salt to taste

For the filling
¾ cup boiled sweet corn kernels (*makai ke dane*)
½ tsp finely chopped garlic
½ cup finely chopped capsicum
1 tbsp chopped celery
1 cup grated mozzarella cheese or cooking cheese
1 tbsp cream
1 tsp butter
Salt and pepper to taste

For the garnish

1 tsp chopped parsley

For the filling

1. Heat the butter in a pan, add the garlic and sauté for a few seconds.
2. Add the sweet corn, capsicum and celery and sauté for 2 more minutes.
3. Remove from the fire, add the cheese, cream, salt and pepper, mix well and keep aside.

How to proceed

1. Make criss-cross slits on the top of the boiled potatoes.
2. Press the potatoes from the base to open up the slits and to make a cavity for the filling.
3. Sprinkle salt on the potatoes and fill with the filling mixture.
4. Bake in a pre-heated oven at 200°C (400°F) for 4 to 5 minutes or until the cheese has melted.

   Serve hot garnished with the parsley.

Handy tip : Instead of boiled potatoes, you could wrap them in aluminium foil and bake at 160°C (320°F) for about 30 minutes or till done.

❧ *Corn Panki* ❧

This novel snack retains the lovely aroma of the banana leaves in which the pankis are cooked. Topped with dollops of butter and green chutney, really no one can eat just one!

Preparation time: 10 minutes.   Cooking time:15 minutes.   Serves 4.

6 tender sweet corncobs (*peela bhutta*)
2 tbsp plain flour (*maida*)
2 tbsp semolina (*rawa*)
1 tbsp chopped coriander
2 tsps finely chopped green chillies
¼ tsp soda bi-carb
2 tbsp fresh curds (*dahi*)
2 tsps oil
Salt to taste

Other ingredients
1 banana leaf

To serve
Melted butter
Green chutney

1. Grate the corn cobs.
2. Add the remaining ingredients and mix well. Keep aside.
3. Cut the banana leaf into small squares of approx. 100 mm. (4") diameter.
4. Apply a little oil on all the leaf squares. Keep aside.
5. Spread a little mixture in a thin layer on some leaf squares.
6. Put another greased leaf square on top so as to cover the batter.
7. Cook on a *tava* (griddle) until light brown spots appear on top of the leaf squares. Serve hot with melted butter and green chutney.

❧ *Grilled Corn Toast* ❧

Think beyond plain cheese for your grilled toast. The versatile sweet corn tastes amazing in toast as well.
Serve with Tabasco sauce to complete the lovely experience.

Preparation time: 10 minutes.   Cooking time:10 minutes.   Serves 4.

8 bread slices
½ cup cooked sweet corn kernels (*makai ke dane*)
2 tbsp milk
¼ cup grated cheese
¼ cup chopped onions
1 tsp chopped green chillies
¼ cup chopped tomatoes, deseeded and without pulp
½ tsp mustard (*rai / sarson*) powder
2 tbsp butter, softened
1 tbsp oil
Salt to taste

To serve
Tabasco sauce

1. Mix the milk, cheese and butter in a bowl. Keep aside.
2. Heat the oil in a non-stick pan, add the onions and green chillies and sauté till the onions turn translucent.
3. Add the tomatoes, corn, mustard powder and salt and mix well. Keep aside.
4. Toast the bread slices. On one side of the bread slice, spread a little of the above mixture.
5. Place the bread slices below the grill for a few minutes.
6. When toasted, cut into pieces and serve hot with Tabasco sauce.

Mini Series by *Tarla Dalal*

7 Dinner Menus

Forever Young Diet

Nutritious Recipes for Pregnancy

Healthy Subzis

High Blood Pressure Cookbook

Low Calorie Sweets

Good Food for Diabetes

Healthy Snacks for Kids

Iron Rich Recipes

Low Cholesterol Recipes

Healthy Juices

Healthy Breakfast

Healthy Snacks

Healthy Soups & Salads

Calcium Rich Recipes

Home Remedies

Fast Foods made Healthy